Rise Again!

A 30-Day Devotional for Renewal, Strength, and Starting Over

GBENGA SHOWUNMI

Rise Again

Published by Cornerstone Publishing

A Division of Cornerstone Creativity Group LLC
Info@thecornerstonepublishers.com
www.thecornerstonepublishers.com

Author's Contact

To book the author to speak at your next event or to order bulk copies of this book, please, use the information below:

pastorshow@gmail.com | gbengashowunmi.com

Printed in the United States of America.

Proverbs 24:16 (NIV)

For though the righteous fall
seven times, they **rise again**,
but the wicked stumble when
calamity strikes.

CONTENTS

PREFACE

There are seasons in life when everything feels stalled. You're not where you used to be, but you're also not where you're meant to be. You pray, but heaven feels silent. You take steps, but nothing seems to change. You dream, but fear and fatigue challenge you at every turn.

This devotional is for that season.

Rise Again is not just a collection of positive thoughts; it's a spiritual nudge, a divine challenge, and a prophetic journey designed to get you unstuck, motivated, and back on the path to your purpose. Whether you're recovering from failure, navigating grief, rebuilding after loss, or simply tired of waiting, this 30-day devotional is your invitation to rise again.

Scripture says, *"Though the righteous fall seven times, they rise again"* (Proverbs 24:16, NIV). Rising is not only possible; it's promised. Isaiah 60:1 declares, *"Arise, shine, for your light has come, and the glory of the Lord rises upon you."* This is more than mere survival; it's your divine call to stand, shine, and soar.

Each entry is crafted to stir your faith, acknowledge your pain, and awaken your calling. You'll find scripture-based reflections, real-life stories, breakthrough declarations, and prayers that bring you face-to-face with the God who still raises people from ruins.

You were not born to settle. You were not created to remain stuck. You were designed to rise again and again until you become everything heaven intended for you.

Let's embark on this journey together. Let this be your rise, for real, for good, for glory.

Day 1

THE CALL TO RISE

Scripture:

"Arise, shine; for your light has come! And the glory of the Lord is risen upon you."

— ISAIAH 60:1 (NKJV)

REFLECTION:

The first word is **"Arise."** Not *rest*, not *wait*, not *wish*, but *arise*. That's a call to action. God's instruction to you is not dependent on your feelings; it's based on what He has placed within you. He sees beyond your weariness, your fear, and your disappointments. He sees your *glory potential*.

Yes, you've faced challenges. Life has knocked you down. You've had silent seasons where it felt like your prayers bounced off the ceiling. You've wondered if your story could ever change. But here's the truth: **Heaven is calling you to rise, again.**

This is not just motivation; it's a prophetic command.

God never speaks without the power behind His word. When He said, "Let there be light," light had no choice but to appear. When He says, "Arise," you have divine support to stand, even in your weakness. You don't rise because you feel strong; you rise because His Word declares it.

Every rising begins with obedience. You don't need to see the entire picture. Just take that first step. Stand in your spirit. Stand in your faith. Stand in your purpose.

Not long ago, a discouraged young man walked into my office after enduring his third layoff in two years. He was disheartened and felt like a failure. But before he left, I asked him one question: "What would happen if you rose up anyway?" That conversation ignited a turnaround. He revived an old business idea, trusted God, and today he's employing others. His rise began the day he chose to say yes.

You are not forgotten. You are not disqualified.

This is your call. This is your moment.

Arise!

DECLARATIONS:

👤 Say these aloud in faith:

- I arise from every limitation and step into my God-given destiny.

- I shake off every weight, fear, and failure; my time has come.

- The glory of the Lord is rising upon me, and I will not miss it.

- I am not stuck; I am sent. I am not finished; I am being formed.

- I walk boldly into today with purpose, courage, and clarity.

- Every invisible chain is breaking off me in Jesus' name.

- I am rising, not by power or might, but by the Spirit of the Lord.

PRAYER:

Father, thank You for calling me to rise. I confess that there have been times I felt buried, forgotten, and too broken to move. But today, I respond to Your call. I say **yes**—yes to Your timing, yes to Your power, yes to Your glory. Empower me to take bold steps this week. Let the fire of Your Word burn away fear and hesitation. Let me arise and shine as You intended me to. In Jesus' name, amen.

Day 2

STUCK BUT NOT FORSAKEN

Scripture:

"The righteous cry out, and the Lord hears, and delivers them out of all their troubles."

— PSALM 34:17 (NKJV)

REFLECTION:

Being stuck doesn't mean you've been abandoned. It simply means you're in between: between where you've been and where God is taking you. Often, it's in those tight, in-between spaces that God does His deepest work.

You may feel like nothing is moving. Your prayers sound like echoes. Your efforts don't seem to yield results. But remember, God sees you. He hears every cry. He is not ignoring you. In fact, He often performs His most powerful miracles in hidden places.

Joseph was stuck in a prison, forgotten by men but not by God. David was stuck in a cave, but he was still anointed. Ruth was stuck in widowhood and poverty, but she was on the path to divine favor. Even Jesus was stuck in a grave, but only for three days.

There was a season when I connected with a woman who described her life as a spiritual holding. Nothing was working. Her dreams were on hold. But every night, she wrote in her journal, "God hasn't forgotten me." That simple act kept her spirit alive. Two years later, she launched a nonprofit that now serves hundreds. Her "stuck" season was not punishment; it was preparation.

You may feel stuck today, but you are not forsaken. Don't judge your future by your present circumstances. God is still writing your story. Keep praying. Keep moving, even if it's only in faith. Your season of deliverance and breakthrough is coming!

DECLARATIONS:

Declare these with boldness:

- I may feel stuck, but I am not forgotten.

- God is with me in this place, and He is working behind the scenes.

- I will not give up; I am coming out stronger.

- My situation is temporary, but my calling is eternal.

- What looks like a delay is part of my divine preparation.

- I trust God's timing over my timeline.

- I am moving from stuck to soaring by the grace of God.

PRAYER:

Lord, thank You that even in seasons when I feel stuck, You are still near. Help me not to misinterpret delay as denial or isolation as rejection. Teach me to wait with faith and move with wisdom. Remind me that You are a Deliverer and that nothing is too hard for You. Give me eyes to see purpose in this place and the strength to believe until I break through. In Jesus' name, amen.

Day 3

WHEN HOPE
IS BURIED

Scripture:

"Can these bones live?" So I answered, "O Lord God, You know."

— EZEKIEL 37:3 (NKJV)

REFLECTION:

Have you ever looked at a situation so lifeless, so hopeless, that you whispered to yourself, *"There's no coming back from this"*? That's likely how the prophet Ezekiel felt when God brought him to a valley filled with dry bones—bones that were not just dead, but *very dry*. There was no sign of life, and every trace of hope seemed buried.

Sometimes life feels exactly like that. A relationship ends, a dream fades, and years pass without seeing what you believed God for come to fruition. At first, you prayed. Then you waited. Eventually, you stopped hoping. Because hope deferred can leave the heart sick.

But here's the truth: even when hope is buried, God is not finished.

A pastor once confided in me about the pain of shutting down his church after years of struggling and dwindling attendance. He told me, "I buried that dream. I even told God I was done." Two years later, through an unexpected connection, he was invited to lead a church in another city. Today, that church is thriving, and the very message he once gave up on is transforming lives. He said to me, "It wasn't over. I just couldn't see the life that was still in the bones."

Your situation may seem dead, but God is not intimidated by dry bones. He still speaks to lifeless places. His breath still revives. His Word still restores. Don't walk away from what God is ready to resurrect.

If He could raise Lazarus, open Sarah's womb, and restore Job's fortune, He can breathe life into your buried hope.

DECLARATIONS:

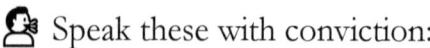 Speak these with conviction:

- I believe again. I choose faith over despair.

- Every dry place in my life is receiving divine breath.

- I call forth purpose, potential, and promise from dead places.

- My hope is not in what I see, but in the Word of the Lord.

- God is resurrecting buried dreams and long-lost prayers.

- I refuse to settle in the valley; resurrection power is at work in me.

- I declare: these bones shall live!

PRAYER:

Father, I thank You that no situation is beyond Your reach. Where I've lost hope, restore it. Where I've buried dreams, speak again. Teach me to prophesy to what looks dead. Let Your Word be louder than my disappointment. I give You every valley, every dry bone, every abandoned prayer. Breathe on it again. Resurrect what I thought was over. In Jesus' name, amen.

Day 4

THE BREAKING POINT

Scripture:

"Unless a grain of wheat falls into the ground and dies, it remains alone; but if it dies, it produces much grain."

— JOHN 12:24 (NKJV)

REFLECTION:

No one enjoys the breaking point. It's uncomfortable, painful, and often misunderstood. But if we're honest, it's also where most breakthroughs begin.

God often does His greatest work in us when everything around us seems to be falling apart.

The breaking point is not proof that God has abandoned you; it's often proof that He's preparing you. Before there can be multiplication, there must be surrender. Before the resurrection, there is always a death. The seed must fall before it can rise.

Jesus spoke this truth when He said a grain of wheat must fall to the ground and die before it can produce fruit. He wasn't just talking about Himself; He was showing us the pattern of spiritual growth. If it feels like something in you is dying, it may be that God is planting you for something greater.

In a tough counseling session, a young man poured out his heart about losing nearly everything in one month. With tears in his eyes, he said, "It feels like God is crushing me." I gently replied, "Maybe He's not crushing you. Maybe He's planting you."

You may be in a season of pressure, confusion, or loss. But God is not wasting your pain. What's breaking in you is making way for what's about to break through. Trust the process. The breaking point is not the end; it's a setup for divine multiplication.

DECLARATIONS:

Say these aloud with faith:

- My breaking is not the end; it's the beginning of something greater.

- God is using this pain to prepare me for purpose.

- I will not quit. I will be fruitful.

- I trust the process even when I don't understand the plan.

- What the enemy meant for evil, God is turning for my good.

- I am being formed, not forsaken.

- My breaking point will become my breakthrough testimony.

PRAYER:

Lord, I bring You my broken pieces. I may not understand this season, but I choose to trust You in it. Let the crushing produce oil. Let the pressure birth purpose. Help me endure with grace and rise with power. In Jesus' name, amen.

Day 5

WHY GOD ALLOWS SETBACKS

Scripture:

"And we know that all things work together for good to those who love God, to those who are the called according to His purpose."

— ROMANS 8:28 (NKJV)

REFLECTION:

Setbacks are never fun. They can be painful, confusing, and deeply frustrating. You start a project with excitement, only to watch it stall. You apply for a promotion, only to be passed over. You dream big, only to find yourself hitting invisible walls. In moments like these, it's easy to ask, "God, where are You in this?"

The truth is, God is often working *through* the very setbacks we're trying to pray away. Just because the path is disrupted doesn't mean the purpose is canceled. Sometimes the delay is divine. Sometimes the closed door is God's protection. And sometimes, the detour is the real training ground for destiny.

Joseph experienced setbacks through betrayal, slavery, and false accusations. Yet every step of his painful journey was leading him closer to the palace. What others meant to destroy him, God used to position him.

Some time ago, a woman shared how she had been denied entry into a graduate program she'd spent years preparing for. She was devastated. But that forced delay pushed her into a temporary internship where she discovered a different passion, one that led to an international leadership role she never saw coming. Years later, she told me, "God rerouted me, but He didn't reject me."

Your setback is not a sign that God has changed His mind about you. It may be the very tool He's using to shape, protect, or prepare you. Don't misinterpret divine redirection as rejection. God's plan is still on course, even when your timeline isn't.

DECLARATIONS:

Declare these with conviction:

- My setback is not my end; it's part of God's strategy.

- I trust God even when the way is unclear.

- What looks like delay is leading to divine alignment.

- I am not rejected; I am being rerouted.

- God is working all things together for my good.

- I will rise stronger because of this season.

- My purpose will not be aborted by temporary disappointments.

PRAYER:

Father, thank You for being present even in the seasons that don't make sense. I surrender every delay, every disappointment, and every "no" I didn't expect. Help me to see setbacks through Your eyes. Teach me to wait with worship and walk with wisdom. Let this season refine me, not define me. I trust Your plan. In Jesus' name, amen.

Day 6

YOUR RISE IS PERSONAL

~

Scripture:

"Fear not, for I have redeemed you; I have called you by your name; You are Mine."

— ISAIAH 43:1 (NKJV)

REFLECTION:

God is not calling you to rise as just another face in a crowd. His call is personal. He doesn't just know your story; He authored it. He doesn't just tolerate your struggles; He walks with you through them. He calls you by name, not by your failures.

It's easy to look at others rising and wonder if God has forgotten you. But comparison is a thief, and silence is not absence. God's timing for your life is strategic. When He calls you to rise, it's not a copy of someone else's breakthrough; it's a tailored elevation rooted in your divine assignment.

After a Sunday service, a young woman shared how overlooked she felt in her career and relationships. But that morning, during worship, she felt the Holy Spirit whisper her name; just her name. That whisper changed everything. "I knew I was seen," she said. I knew my rise was coming." Six months later, she was leading a new department at her job.

Your rise is not generic. It's God-ordained, heaven-authored, and time-stamped. You are not one of many; you are one of one. And when God calls your name, nothing and no one can stop your rise.

DECLARATIONS:

 Speak these out loud with faith:

- God knows me, sees me, and calls me by name.

- My rise is personal, purposeful, and powerful.

- I am not forgotten; I am chosen.

- I break free from the trap of comparison.

- My story is significant, and my time is coming.

- I will not settle for less than what God wrote about me.

- I rise with clarity, courage, and conviction.

PRAYER:

Father, thank You for calling me by name. I am not invisible to You. You know my fears, my delays, and my hidden prayers. Lord, Help me to stop comparing my journey with others and start embracing my unique path. Let me rise into the purpose You designed just for me. In Jesus' name, amen.

Day 7

THE POWER OF PERSPECTIVE

Scripture:

"As he thinks in his heart, so is he."

PROVERBS 23:7A (NKJV)

REFLECTION:

Your perspective can either confine you or set you free. How you *view* yourself, your circumstances, and your faith will always influence how you move forward. If you see yourself as defeated, you may stop fighting. But if you recognize that even in struggles, you are still called, chosen, and destined, everything can change.

The Bible is filled with stories of individuals who had to shift their perspective before stepping into their true calling. Gideon viewed himself as the least in his family, but God saw him as a mighty warrior. The spies saw giants, while Joshua and Caleb recognized opportunity. David viewed Goliath as a chance for God to demonstrate His power. Your perception shapes your journey.

During a prison outreach, I met a man whose mindset had shifted completely after years behind bars. He shared, "For a long time, I identified with my past mistakes. But one day, I began to see myself as God sees me." That change in perspective transformed his life. Today, he owns a business, and his life changed the moment his mindset did.

The breakthrough you're seeking may not start with external changes; it might begin with a renewal of your mind. Don't let the enemy deceive you about your identity. Don't allow past pain to define who you are today. See through the lens of faith, and you'll begin to rise from within.

DECLARATIONS:

Speak these aloud with conviction:

- I see myself the way God sees me— redeemed, equipped, and rising.

- I break every agreement with lies and limitations.

- My mind is renewed daily by God's Word.

- I choose faith over fear and victory over victimhood.

- God's perspective is my perspective.

- I am not defined by my past; I am who God has called me to be.

- I rise with a renewed mind and unstoppable vision.

PRAYER:

Lord, help me to see clearly—not just with my eyes, but with my heart. Teach me to think like a victor, not a victim. Reveal any false beliefs I've held and replace them with Your truth. Let my perspective align with Your promises. As my mind is renewed, may my life be transformed. In Jesus' name, amen.

Day 8

BREAKING LIMITING BELIEFS

Scripture:

"Do not be conformed to this world, but be transformed by the renewing of your mind, that you may prove what is that good and acceptable and perfect will of God."

ROMANS 12:2 (NKJV)

REFLECTION:

The greatest barriers holding many people back are not physical; they are mental. It's not just the events in your life that keep you stuck; it's the beliefs you form because of them. Limiting beliefs are deceptive narratives that often sound like truth.

They stem from past wounds, repeated failures, fear, or rejection, whispering discouraging thoughts like, "You'll never be enough," "You'll always lag behind," or "People like you don't succeed."

But God's Word can demolish those lies.

Real breakthrough begins with renewing your mind. When your beliefs change, your actions will follow. When you stop agreeing with the enemy's narrative and start aligning with God's truth, you'll notice shifts in your thinking and life.

Years ago, a young woman I mentored struggled to believe she was truly leadership material. She was too broken to lead. Despite having the calling, passion, and gifts, she saw herself as unqualified. After months of exploring Scripture and praying together, she confronted that lie. Today, she not only leads but also empowers others who once believed the same falsehood.

You cannot rise if your mind is anchored to a false identity. It's time to dismantle the lies and embrace the truth. Your thoughts shape your reality. God has called you to greatness—believe it, declare it, and walk in it.

DECLARATIONS:

Declare these in faith and freedom:

- I break every limiting belief that has held me back.

- I am not defined by my past, pain, or mistakes; I am who God says I am.

- My mind is being renewed, and my life is being transformed.

- I reject every lie that claims I'm not enough.

- I embrace truth, power, purpose, and progress.

- God's Word is my mirror and my guide.

- I rise with a renewed identity and unshakeable faith.

PRAYER:

Father, thank You for revealing the lies that have limited me. I renounce every belief that You didn't place in me. Flood my mind with Your truth and reshape how I perceive myself. Help me walk boldly into who You've called me to be. Break every chain of fear, failure, and false identity. I choose to believe again. I choose to rise. In Jesus' name, amen.

Day 9

CONQUERING FEAR

Scripture:

"For God has not given us a spirit of fear, but of power and of love and of a sound mind."

2 TIMOTHY 1:7 (NKJV)

REFLECTION:

Fear is a thief. It creeps in, whispers lies, and robs you of the courage to follow God. It magnifies giants, makes risks seem insurmountable, and renders dreams unrealistic. Fear doesn't always present itself as panic; sometimes it masquerades as hesitation, overthinking, or playing it safe.

But here's the truth: fear does not come from God. It's not your inheritance or your portion. The

Scriptures refer to it as a *spirit*, meaning it doesn't just visit; it attempts to stay. Like any spirit not of God, it must be expelled.

Courage isn't the absence of fear; it's obedience in spite of it. It's listening to God's voice louder than the fear inside your head. When God prompts you to rise, move, build, speak, or go, fear will always attempt to argue. But faith responds.

A businessman once admitted to me how fear of repeating his father's failures kept him from launching his business for years. He would plan, prepare, and then freeze. One day, he realized he was succumbing to a fear that wasn't even his. That moment of clarity broke something within him. He launched his business, and while the journey wasn't easy, he now leads a thriving company and helps other men confront their fears.

You will never fully rise until you boldly conquer fear. And you won't conquer fear by playing small. You overcome it by leaning into God's truth, embracing His power, and moving forward, even if your knees are shaking.

DECLARATIONS:

Say these with passion and determination:

- Fear has no place in my life; I walk in divine courage.

- I have power, love, and a sound mind through Christ.

- I silence every voice of fear with the voice of faith.

- I was not created to play small; I was born to rise.

- My destiny is greater than my comfort zone.

- I will not fear failure, rejection, or delay.

- I rise above fear and walk in supernatural boldness.

PRAYER:

Father, I thank You that fear is not from You. Today, I confront every fear that has held me back: fear of failure, fear of rejection, and fear of inadequacy. I renounce these fears and receive Your power, love, and clarity. Let courage rise within me. Teach me to obey You boldly, even when fear looms. I will not bow to fear. I rise in faith. In Jesus' name, amen.

THE STRONGHOLD OF SHAME

Scripture:

"Instead of your shame you shall have double honor, and instead of confusion they shall rejoice in their portion."

— ISAIAH 61:7A (NKJV)

REFLECTION:

Shame often thrives in silence. It doesn't always shout; sometimes, it quietly lingers in the background, convincing you that your mistakes disqualify you from your purpose. It causes you to second-guess yourself, avoid certain prayers, dodge new opportunities, and hide from the very things

God is calling you to do.

But shame is not from God. Condemnation is the enemy's tool to keep you tied to your past. In contrast, grace is God's invitation for you to step boldly into your future.

The cross didn't merely cover your sin; it also crushed your shame. Jesus didn't just die for your actions; He died to restore your self-image. Shame tries to convince you that you must earn your way back into God's favor. However, God beckons you, *"Come boldly."*

One Sunday during communion, a man who had once walked away from ministry found the courage to say yes again. For years, he sat in the pews, too ashamed to lead again. But one Sunday during communion, something shifted within him. He embraced God's forgiveness and chose to forgive himself. He whispered, "God, if You can still use me, I'm available." Today, the rest is history!

You don't have to remain hidden. God wants to redeem your story. Where shame says, "Stay down," grace says, "Rise up." God is not just restoring you in private; He is preparing to honor you publicly.

DECLARATIONS:

Declare these boldly and daily:

- I am not what I did; I am who God says I am.

- Shame has no power over me; I walk in grace and freedom.

- I refuse to let the past silence my purpose.

- I receive double honor for every place I once felt shame.

- I am forgiven, restored, and called.

- My life is a testimony of God's mercy.

- I rise free, clean, and confident in Christ.

PRAYER:

Lord, thank You for covering my shame and clothing me in righteousness. I lay every regret, every failure, and every hidden weight at Your feet. Break the power of shame in my heart and mind. Help me walk boldly in the identity You've given me. Where I once felt unworthy, fill me with holy confidence. I rise as a new creation. In Jesus' name, amen.

Day 11

THE WALLS
MUST FALL

Scripture:

"By faith the walls of Jericho fell down after they were encircled for seven days."

— HEBREWS 11:30 (NKJV)

REFLECTION:

Every destiny has its Jericho—those situations that seem tall, fortified, and unmoved. You pray, you fast, you march, but it feels like nothing is changing. The wall seems to mock your obedience, and the enemy taunts your persistence. But if God says it must fall, it will.

Walls don't fall due to human strength; they fall when faith meets divine timing. Israel marched around Jericho for seven days in silence before the victory shout. It may sound strange, but God was teaching them, and us, that breakthrough comes from obedience, not noise.

Sometimes God will ask you to do things that don't make logical sense. Keep marching anyway. Keep showing up. Keep circling that promise in prayer, worship, and prophetic obedience. You may not see the cracks yet, but heaven is counting your steps.

I once prayed with a woman who was believing for a child after ten years of waiting. Every medical report felt like a wall. But she refused to stop marching. Every night, she would walk her hallway declaring, "My God is faithful." In year eleven, she conceived and later gave birth to twins. The wall fell.

Walls don't mean it is over for you; they are opportunities for God to reveal His power. And when they fall, they fall fast. So don't stop marching. Your next lap might be the one that brings everything down.

DECLARATIONS:

Declare these like a warrior:

- Every wall standing between me and my breakthrough is falling.

- I march by faith, not by sight.

- God is fighting for me, and nothing is impossible with Him.

- My obedience is my weapon.

- I will not grow weary in well-doing.

- The walls may look strong, but my God is stronger.

- I rise with faith that moves obstacles.

PRAYER:

Lord, I thank You that no wall is too big for You to bring down. Strengthen me to keep moving forward, even when it feels repetitive. Remind me that every act of obedience counts. I trust Your timing and Your ways. Let every Jericho in my life fall at the sound of my faith. I rise with confidence, knowing You've already secured the victory. In Jesus' name, amen.

Day 12

FAITH UNDER PRESSURE

~~~~~~

Scripture:

"We are hard-pressed on every side, yet not crushed; we are perplexed, but not in despair."

2 CORINTHIANS 4:8 (NKJV)

REFLECTION:

Pressure is a part of the journey. It doesn't signify weakness; it signifies that you're alive and being prepared for more. The people God uses most powerfully often endure the greatest pressure. They don't rejoice in pain, but they understand that pressure reveals what's real.

When your faith is under pressure, your beliefs become clearer. It's easy to trust God when everything is going smoothly, but true faith is forged in the fire, when you face demands, decisions, and delays. Faith under pressure lasts and yields fruit.

In a moment of exhaustion, a single mother juggling jobs, classes, and church came to me for prayer. She felt overwhelmed by it all. "Why does it feel like everything is closing in?" she asked. I reminded her that diamonds are formed under pressure, just like leaders. Today, she is debt-free and graduated with honors. The pressure didn't break her; it refined her.

If you're feeling pressure today, don't think God is far away. He's closer than you realize. Let the pressure lead you to prayer, not panic. Allow it to stretch your trust and strengthen your spirit. The oil only comes when the olive is crushed. But once it flows, it brings healing and light.

DECLARATIONS:

Say these with conviction, even through the pressure:

- I may be pressed, but I will not be crushed.

- God is with me in every high and low moment.

- My faith is growing stronger under pressure.

- I will not panic; I will pray and trust.

- This pressure is producing something powerful in me.

- I will emerge from this refined, not ruined.

- I rise above stress and stand in supernatural strength.

PRAYER:

Father, You see the pressure I'm under. Some days I feel overwhelmed and worn out. But I declare today that I will not be crushed. You are my strength and my peace. Let this pressure produce something eternal in me. Teach me to lean on You when I want to run. Let my faith hold strong and my heart stay soft. In Jesus' name, amen.

Day 13

FIGHT FOR
YOUR MIND

Scripture:

"Casting down arguments and every high thing that exalts itself against the knowledge of God, bringing every thought into captivity to the obedience of Christ."

2 CORINTHIANS 10:5 (NKJV)

REFLECTION:

The greatest battlefield in your life isn't your finances, your relationships, or your circumstances; it's your mind. That's where the enemy does his finest work: planting seeds of fear, doubt, insecurity, and defeat. If he can convince you to believe a lie, he can make you live as if it's true.

That's why Scripture tells us to take every thought captive. You can't be passive in this war. You must fight for your mind every day.

The enemy doesn't have to take your destiny if he can take your focus. That's why some people are gifted but paralyzed, called but distracted, anointed but anxious. Their minds are under siege.

At a conference, I met a man wrestling with crippling mental torment that nearly stole his calling. "Every time I was about to step out," he said, "I'd be flooded with thoughts like, 'Who do you think you are?' or 'You're not ready.'" Through consistent prayer, fasting, and speaking God's Word aloud daily, he broke that pattern. Today, he's preaching the very messages he once doubted he had the strength to speak.

The enemy doesn't get to have the last word. You do. It's time to stop entertaining thoughts that don't align with your destiny. If it doesn't sound like something God would say about you, *don't let it live in your head.*

This is your mind. Guard it. Train it. Fight for it. Win in it.

DECLARATIONS:

Speak these aloud until they become your mindset:

- I take every thought captive and make it obey Christ.

- My mind is protected, purified, and peaceful.

- I reject fear, shame, and confusion; I have the mind of Christ.

- No lie can live in me; I walk in truth and clarity.

- I am mentally strong, spiritually alert, and emotionally whole.

- I fight from victory, not for it.

- I rise with a focused mind and a fearless heart.

PRAYER:

Lord, thank You for giving me authority over my thoughts. I repent for every time I've agreed with fear, doubt, or lies. Today, I cast them down. I receive Your peace, Your clarity, and Your truth. Train my mind to obey Your Word and reject every toxic pattern. In Jesus' name, amen.

Day 14

FROM SURVIVING TO SOARING

~~~~~~

Scripture:

"But those who wait on the Lord shall renew their strength; they shall mount up with wings like eagles, they shall run and not be weary, they shall walk and not faint."

ISAIAH 40:31 (NKJV)

REFLECTION:

There's a difference between surviving and soaring. Surviving is about making it through the day. Soaring is about rising above it. Surviving keeps you in maintenance mode. Soaring launches you into momentum.

Too many believers have settled for survival. They're spiritually breathing, but not flying. They're not dead, but they're not really living either. But God did not bring you this far to leave you circling the same mountain. He created you to soar.

When Isaiah said you would "mount up with wings like eagles," he wasn't talking about a good feeling during worship. He was describing a spiritual shift. Eagles don't flap, they soar. They rise above storms by riding the wind, not fighting it. That's what happens when you stop trying to do life in your own strength and start relying on God's.

A woman once told me that after years of hardship, she had forgotten how to dream. She'd gone through divorce, betrayal, and financial hardship. "I was always surviving," she said, "but never really living." It wasn't until she surrendered her control and embraced God's strength that her life shifted. She went from waiting tables to leading a women's empowerment organization. Her survival season gave way to a soaring testimony.

You were not born to flap around in fear, fatigue, and frustration. The wind of God is blowing. Let Him carry you higher. Stop surviving. It's time to soar.

DECLARATIONS:

Say these with the confidence of someone born to rise:

- I am not just surviving; I am soaring by the grace of God.

- I rise above fear, fatigue, and failure.

- I refuse to stay stuck in cycles; I embrace a divine momentum.

- God is renewing my strength each day.

- I rise with the strength of an eagle.

- I was born to live fully, lead boldly, and love deeply.

- I soar into purpose, power, and peace.

PRAYER:

Father, I thank You that I'm not meant to merely survive. You created me to soar. Forgive me for settling into survival mode. Today, I choose to rise. Let Your strength lift me above every storm, and let Your wind carry me where my own wings cannot. I receive grace for forward movement. I leave behind delay and embrace my destiny. In Jesus' name, amen.

Day 15

DESIGNED FOR DESTINY

Scripture:

"Before I formed you in the womb I knew you; before you were born I sanctified you; I ordained you a prophet to the nations."

— JEREMIAH 1:5 (NKJV)

REFLECTION:

You weren't created by accident. You are not a mistake. Long before your first breath, God wrote your purpose into His grand design. You were crafted with intention, equipped for a unique mission, and meant to leave an impact.

Jeremiah felt unprepared when God called him. He saw himself as small, unqualified, and uncertain. But God didn't expect him to feel ready. He reminded him that he was *formed*, *known*, and *appointed*. In essence, "You're not starting from scratch. I've already woven destiny into your being."

The same holds true for you. Your background doesn't negate your calling. Your pain doesn't nullify your purpose. Everything you've experienced is part of your preparation. Destiny isn't something you earn; it's something you embrace.

In conversation with a man who had drifted from job to job, he shared how purpose finally caught up with him. "I didn't know who I was," he shared. "But the day I asked God to reveal what He saw in me, that was the start of something new." That prayer led him to a calling where he teaches at-risk youth. He found his path, and he's been thriving ever since.

You don't have to invent your purpose. You simply need to *discover* it. God has already placed it within you. Stop going in circles and start running your race. You were designed for destiny.

DECLARATIONS:

Declare these boldly:

- I was created on purpose and for a purpose.

- God knew me, formed me, and called me.

- My identity is rooted in heaven's plan, not life's labels.

- I am not random; I am relevant and necessary.

- I embrace my assignment with confidence and clarity.

- My past is preparation, not disqualification.

- I rise into the destiny I was born for.

PRAYER:

Father, thank You for shaping me with purpose. I silence every voice that says I'm not enough. Help me see myself through Your eyes. Reveal the assignment You've placed within me. I release confusion and comparison, and I say yes to the journey You've called me to run. Let me walk daily in my destiny, guided by Your voice and empowered by Your Spirit. In Jesus' name, amen.

Day 16

PURPOSE IN THE PAIN

———— ❦ ————

Scripture:

"But as for you, you meant evil against me; but God meant it for good, in order to bring it about as it is this day, to save many people alive."

— GENESIS 50:20 (NKJV)

REFLECTION:

Pain rarely feels purposeful while you're enduring it. It can seem unjust, unnecessary, and even overwhelming. But when God is involved, pain is never wasted. What the enemy intended to break you, God can use to build you.

Joseph's story exemplifies this. He was betrayed by his brothers, sold into slavery, falsely accused, and forgotten in prison. Yet, when he eventually rose to power, he could look back and say, *"God used it all."* What once seemed like detours were actually routes to his destiny. The same is true for you.

That heartbreak? That betrayal? That delay? God didn't cause it, but He can redeem it. Pain transforms into purpose when it's placed in God's hands.

A man who lost his job of over two decades once shared how he had to learn success all over again. He struggled with discouragement and fear of starting over in midlife. For a long time, he withdrew, feeling unqualified. But gradually, as he leaned into God through prayer and the Word, something shifted. He didn't chase a new title or public recognition. He simply rebuilt his life with dignity and peace. Today, he works at a smaller company, earning less than before, but living with a joy he never had. "I used to think success was about climbing," he told me. "Now I see it's about becoming."

Don't waste your pain by hiding it or rushing through it. Let God use it to transform you. Sometimes, purpose in pain isn't about changing the world; it's about allowing God to change *you*.

If you're still in it, hold on; transformation is happening.

DECLARATIONS:

Speak these in faith:

1. My pain has a purpose, and God is using it for my good.

2. I will not let what hurt me stop what God wants to do through me.

3. Every scar is becoming a story of grace and glory.

4. What the enemy meant for evil, God is turning around.

5. I rise with healing in my hands and purpose in my steps.

6. I refuse to waste my pain; I offer it to God.

7. My life is a testimony in progress.

PRAYER:

Lord, I bring You every painful place in my life. I trust You to redeem what I don't yet understand. Help me see the purpose beyond the pain. Teach me to comfort others with the same comfort You've given me. Use my wounds to bring healing to someone else. I believe You are working all things for my good. In Jesus' name, amen.

Day 17

POWER TO
START OVER

❧ ⚬❦⚬❧ ❧

Scripture:

*"Though your beginning was small, yet your
latter end would increase abundantly."*

— JOB 8:7 (NKJV)

REFLECTION:

Starting over can feel like defeat. It can seem like
failure or being left behind. But with God, starting
over isn't a setback; it's a divine restart. It's not
the end of your story; it's the beginning of a new
chapter.

Sometimes, God allows things to fall apart so He
can rebuild with greater glory. Job lost everything,

but he didn't succumb to despair. He drew closer to God, and in the end, he received double. Ruth started anew in a foreign land with only her faith and ended up in the lineage of Jesus. Peter denied Jesus three times, but after his restoration, he became the preacher who launched the early church.

Your fresh start may seem small, but don't judge the future by your current circumstances. Heaven never gives up on what it created. If God allowed the reset, He has already planned for the restoration.

After his business collapsed, a friend of mine whispered a simple but powerful prayer that sparked his comeback. For years, he lived in fear of trying again. But one night, he said, "Lord, if You'll walk with me, I'll rise again." That was the start of his comeback. Today, his second business is thriving. What looked like an ending was actually a reintroduction.

If you're holding back because of past failures, hear this clearly: **you can start again.** And this time, you're not starting from scratch. You're starting from experience, equipped with grace, wisdom, and God's guidance in your life.

DECLARATIONS:

Say these with renewed faith:

- I have the power to begin again, and I will not be afraid.

- My past failure does not cancel my future calling.

- God is the Author of new beginnings, and mine has begun.

- I rise from the ashes with divine strength and strategy.

- I walk boldly into what's next without fear or shame.

- My small beginning will become something great.

- This is not the end; this is my moment to rise again.

PRAYER:

Father, thank You for granting me the opportunity to start over. I let go of fear, failure, and regret. I believe You are doing a new thing in me. Lead me with fresh vision and renewed faith. Where I once stumbled, help me to rise stronger. May this new beginning bring glory to You and healing to others. In Jesus' name, amen.

Day 18

OPPOSITION
IS PROOF

—✦—

Scripture:

"For a great and effective door has opened to me, and there are many adversaries."

1 CORINTHIANS 16:9 (NKJV)

REFLECTION:

Opposition often serves as the strongest confirmation that you're on the right path. Open doors don't always come with red carpets; they often come with resistance. The greater your purpose, the greater the pushback you may encounter.

Paul mentioned that a great door had opened to him, but he also acknowledged the many adversaries that accompanied it. He wasn't complaining; he was clarifying. When God opens a door, the enemy will try to block it—not because the door isn't real, but precisely because it is. Spiritual warfare frequently indicates spiritual movement.

If you're facing unusual resistance, don't pull back. Lean into it. The attack isn't random; it's targeted. Hell doesn't fight what it doesn't fear.

I sat with a couple who shared how every step toward church planting was met with painful opposition. However, everything that could go wrong did: financial setbacks, sickness, and even betrayal from close friends. At one point, they thought about quitting. But instead, they fasted, prayed, and persevered. Today, their church is thriving, and many who once doubted them now serve under their leadership.

Opposition doesn't mean God isn't with you. Sometimes, it's the clearest sign that He is. When you face resistance, don't question your calling; *confirm it*. Your rise is making waves in the spiritual realm. Press through. Purpose is waiting on the other side.

DECLARATIONS:

Speak these out loud with spiritual authority:

- I will not retreat in the face of resistance; I was born to overcome.

- Every attack against me confirms the importance of my assignment.

- I have the grace to stand, the strength to endure, and the power to prevail.

- No weapon formed against me shall prosper.

- I press through every barrier and step fully into open doors.

- God is with me, even when I'm under pressure.

- I rise with confidence; opposition is proof that I'm advancing.

PRAYER:

Lord, thank You for confirming my calling even amidst resistance. Help me discern the enemy's tactics and stand firm in faith. Strengthen me to keep moving forward when warfare intensifies. Let every attack draw me closer to You and deeper into my purpose. I will not fear opposition; I will face it with the full armor of God. In Jesus' name, amen.

Day 19

KEEP BUILDING ANYWAY

Scripture:

"So I answered them, and said to them, 'The God of heaven Himself will prosper us; therefore we His servants will arise and build.'"

— NEHEMIAH 2:20 (NKJV)

REFLECTION:

There will always be reasons to stop building: criticism, distraction, fatigue, and lack of support all test your commitment. But when you know God gave you the blueprint, you don't quit just because it gets hard—you keep building anyway.

Nehemiah rebuilt the walls of Jerusalem despite facing intense resistance. He wasn't a seasoned builder; he was a cupbearer. But when purpose calls, it pushes you beyond your comfort zone. And when opposition arises, it signifies that the work truly matters.

Your God-given assignment might not look impressive to others right now. It could be quiet, hidden, or slow. Remember that obedience builds a legacy. You don't have to feel momentum to keep moving forward. Faithfulness *is* progress.

A pastor I know launched a church with just six people in a storefront, unsure if it would survive. For years, it seemed like no one noticed. He battled discouragement, faced financial challenges, and even questioned whether he had truly heard God. But he kept showing up, praying, and building. Today, that church seats thousands and has planted ministries across three continents. He once told me, "I'm grateful I didn't quit when no one was clapping."

Keep building your business, family, ministry, and whatever God has called you to start. The same God who gave you the vision will also give you the victory. Build through the silence. Build through the setbacks. God is with you in every brick.

DECLARATIONS:

Say these as a builder with bold faith:

- I will not stop building; I am empowered by heaven.

- God's hand is on my assignment, and it will prosper.

- I refuse to be distracted by critics or delays.

- What I'm building will outlast me and bless many.

- Every act of obedience shapes my destiny.

- I am anointed to finish what I've started.

- I rise with faith, strength, and divine focus.

PRAYER:

Father, thank You for trusting me with something worth building. Even when I feel tired, help me stay faithful. Strengthen my hands and set my eyes on the vision, not the noise. I declare that what You've called me to start, I will finish by Your grace. Let the work of my hands bring You glory. In Jesus' name, amen.

Day 20

DOORS, GATES, AND BREAKTHROUGHS

Scripture:

"Lift up your heads, O you gates! And be lifted up, you everlasting doors! And the King of glory shall come in."

PSALM 24:7 (NKJV)

REFLECTION:

In the spiritual realm, doors and gates symbolize access points, transitions, promotions, new seasons, and divine opportunities. Yet, some of those doors don't just open automatically; they require lifting, commanding, and sometimes even fighting for in prayer.

David recognized something in the Spirit that many overlook in the natural: there are gates that obstruct glory, but they must respond to the voice of faith. If you're facing closed doors, stagnant moments, or blocked opportunities, don't panic—prophesy.

Not all delays are denials, and not every closed door is final. Some doors await your partnership with heaven to command access.

A woman testified that the job she was denied came back to her with better pay and position. Feeling crushed, she kept declaring, "This door will open because it's mine." Months later, the company restructured and reopened the position with better pay. She applied again and was hired on the spot. When she entered the building for the first time, she whispered through tears, "The gate lifted."

There are gates in the spirit realm that must respond to your persistence—not because of who you are, but because of *who is with you*. When the King of Glory appears, no barrier can remain standing.

DECLARATIONS:

Speak these as one who walks in spiritual authority:

- I command every locked gate before me to lift.

- Divine doors are opening for me by God's hand.

- I am not delayed; I am right on time in God's plan.

- I will not force open what God has not assigned, but I will not fear what is mine.

- The King of Glory goes before me and makes every crooked path straight.

- I declare breakthrough, favor, and access in every area of my life.

- I rise into new realms of opportunity and divine promotion.

PRAYER:

Lord, You are the King of Glory. Lift every gate, every delay, every hindrance that tries to hold me back. I trust Your timing and follow Your voice. Give me spiritual eyes to discern my season and spiritual boldness to walk through the doors You've ordained. Let breakthrough be my portion and progress be my testimony. In Jesus' name, amen.

Day 21

THE ANOINTING TO RISE

Scripture:

"But you have an anointing from the Holy One, and you know all things."

— 1 JOHN 2:20 (NKJV)

REFLECTION:

You're not rising on motivation alone; you're rising by the anointing. The anointing is the supernatural enablement of God, allowing you to accomplish what you could never achieve on your own.

Throughout Scripture, those who stepped into their purpose weren't necessarily the smartest, strongest, or most connected. They were anointed. David wasn't crowned king because of his résumé; he was anointed while still smelling like sheep. Esther wasn't elevated solely because of her beauty; she carried a divine assignment. Jesus declared in Luke 4:18, *"The Spirit of the Lord is upon Me, because He has anointed Me…"* He understood that His mission would require supernatural assistance.

A man once told me, "I feel like I don't have what it takes," but everything changed when he leaned into the anointing. I looked him in the eye and said, "You're right. You don't. But the anointing does." That truth transformed him. He began to rely on God's presence instead of his own performance, and that shift opened doors he never thought possible.

You are not rising alone. The anointing equips you to speak when you're nervous, build when you feel unqualified, and endure when you're under attack. You don't have to *feel* anointed to *be* anointed. You just have to believe it and walk in it.

DECLARATIONS:

Say these with spiritual authority:

- I carry the anointing of God for my assignment.

- I do not rise by my might, but by His Spirit.

- Every limitation is breaking under the anointing.

- I am equipped, empowered, and endorsed by heaven.

- The anointing gives me clarity, boldness, and breakthrough.

- I will not shrink; I will rise with divine help.

- I walk in fresh oil, fresh power, and fresh purpose.

PRAYER:

Father, thank You for the anointing that rests on my life. Remind me that I'm not rising in my own strength. Help me depend on Your Spirit every step of the way. Anoint my hands for what You've called me to build. Anoint my mind to think clearly. Anoint my voice to speak boldly. Let the oil of Your presence mark everything I do. In Jesus' name, amen.

Day 22

THE WEIGHT
OF GLORY

Scripture

*"For our light affliction, which is but for
a moment, is working for us a far more
exceeding and eternal weight of glory."*

— 2 CORINTHIANS 4:17 (NKJV)

REFLECTION:

Glory has weight. It's not about glitter or applause,
nor is it about a spotlight or platform. The glory
of God is His manifest presence, and carrying it
comes with a cost. However, that cost is never
wasted. Every moment of obedience, every trial
endured, every silent tear—they all contribute to
something eternal.

Paul referred to his affliction as "light," not because it didn't hurt, but because he measured it against the glory it was producing. When you realize that glory is being formed in your wilderness, you stop resenting the process.

I once met a woman who had endured great loss, yet carried God's presence like a mantle. Yet, every time she walked into a room, people felt the presence of God. She never preached, but her life carried weight. One day she said to me, "I didn't ask for this, but I trust that God's glory will come out of it." That's the mindset of those who rise with maturity.

You've endured too much for your life not to carry something powerful. The battles you've fought, the seasons you've faced, and the valleys you've passed through are pressing something eternal into your spirit.

Don't trade lasting glory for temporary gain. Let God finish what He started. Let Him make your life a vessel that carries weight in the spirit. Your affliction has an expiration date, but your glory will echo in eternity.

DECLARATIONS:

Speak these with reverence and strength:

- My pain is producing eternal glory.

- I am not empty; I carry the weight of God's presence.

- I do not live for applause; I live to reveal His glory.

- What I've endured has made me stronger, wiser, and deeper.

- God is turning my affliction into authority.

- I will carry His glory with humility and honor.

- I rise as a vessel of glory, not just victory.

PRAYER:

Lord, thank You that nothing I've been through is wasted. Teach me to carry Your glory with reverence. Let my life reveal Your power, not just my survival. Press into me a depth that reflects heaven. Make me a vessel fit for Your use. Let every trial, every tear, and every triumph work together to carry the weight of Your glory. In Jesus' name, amen.

Day 23

POWER TO
START OVER

━━━━━⚮❦⚮━━━━━

Scripture:

"The latter glory of this house shall be greater than the former, says the Lord of hosts. And in this place, I will give peace..."

— HAGGAI 2:9 (ESV)

REFLECTION:

Some rises don't begin from scratch; they start from ashes. The house has fallen. The dream has died. The chapter has closed. Yet, somehow, there's still a whisper in your spirit: *"This is not the end."*

God specializes in starting over. But He doesn't just restore what was lost; He gives back **better**.

Haggai's prophecy to Israel came when the temple had been destroyed and morale was low. The people wondered, *"Can anything good come from this ruin?"* God assured them, *"The glory that's coming will be greater than what you lost."*

Don't assume God is finished because something failed. He often allows the old to fall so He can raise something stronger, deeper, and more aligned with His purpose.

A man who had experienced bankruptcy, depression, and divorce told me how one retreat reignited his hope. He thought he had nothing left to offer, but during a church retreat, he felt God whisper, "I'm not done with you yet." That moment became his turning point. He began volunteering, rebuilt his business, and eventually remarried. His latter truly is greater than his former.

Don't fear starting over. If God is in it, your rise will be more beautiful, more fruitful, and more purposeful than anything you've seen before. This is not a setback; it's a setup for greater glory.

DECLARATIONS:

Say these with renewed boldness:

- I believe my latter will be greater than my former.

- God is rebuilding me with power, wisdom, and grace.

- I will not fear starting again; I rise with greater purpose.

- Nothing from my past can stop God's plan for my future.

- I receive beauty for ashes and glory for brokenness.

- The best days of my life are still ahead of me.

- I rise from ruins into restoration and divine peace.

PRAYER:

Father, thank You for being the God of new beginnings. Even when I feel like everything has fallen apart, You are still building. I give You every ruin, every disappointment, and every scar. Restore me beyond what I can imagine. Let my latter be greater. Let my life carry a peace and glory that reflects Your faithfulness. In Jesus' name, amen.

Day 24

EMPOWERED BY THE HOLY SPIRIT

———⚬⚬⚬———

Scripture:

"But you shall receive power when the Holy Spirit has come upon you; and you shall be witnesses to Me..."

ACTS 1:8 (NKJV)

REFLECTION:

You weren't meant to rise on your own. You were anointed to rise with **power**—a power that doesn't rely on perfect circumstances but comes from the Spirit of God resting on your life.

When Jesus spoke to the disciples in Acts 1, they were grappling with grief, uncertainty, and fear.

They had witnessed His death, His resurrection, and now His ascension. Yet, He didn't leave them with just memories; He gave them a promise: *"You shall receive power."* This power was meant for rising, leading, and building the Church.

The same is true for you. The Holy Spirit empowers ordinary people to accomplish extraordinary things. You may feel weak, but that weakness is an invitation. When your strength runs out, His begins.

A young woman I prayed with confessed how unqualified she felt, until the Holy Spirit gave her boldness. "I know I'm called," she confided, "but I feel so unqualified." We prayed together for a fresh filling of the Holy Spirit. Weeks later, doors opened, boldness surged, and she stepped into leadership. "It wasn't me," she said. "It was the power of God in me."

The Holy Spirit's anointing breaks yokes, opens doors, and provides what talent, hustle, and effort cannot. You don't need a larger platform; you need a deeper well. Seek the anointing. Walk in it. Rise by it.

DECLARATIONS:

Declare these with spiritual confidence:

- I receive power from the Holy Spirit to rise and fulfill my purpose.

- I will not rely on my own strength; I walk in divine enablement.

- The anointing on my life is opening doors no one can shut.

- I am equipped, empowered, and emboldened by God.

- Every weakness is met with supernatural strength.

- I will rise not by effort alone, but by the Spirit of God.

- I walk in power, authority, and anointing today.

PRAYER:

Holy Spirit, I invite You to fill me anew. I acknowledge that without You, I can do nothing. I surrender every fear, inadequacy, and limitation. Anoint me for the season ahead. Let Your power rest on my life in a fresh way. Empower me to speak, lead, build, and rise into my calling with boldness. In Jesus' name, amen.

Day 25

DIVINE ACCELERATION

Scripture:

"Behold, the days are coming," says the Lord, "when the plowman shall overtake the reaper..."

AMOS 9:13 (NKJV)

REFLECTION:

There are times when God intervenes and accomplishes in one year what would typically take ten. This is what we call **divine acceleration.** It's not just hype; it's heaven's speed. When it touches your life, things start to shift rapidly.

The prophet Amos spoke of a time when sowing and reaping would overlap. This isn't normal or natural; it's supernatural. It means you don't have to wait as long as others have or follow the same rules. When God brings acceleration, delays are broken.

But acceleration also requires alignment. When your heart, mind, and obedience align with God's will, what took others years can happen for you in mere weeks. One encounter, one open door, one divine yes can transform everything.

I once spoke with a man who said God fast-forwarded his purpose after years of stagnation. However, after experiencing a personal revival in his relationship with God, everything changed. Within 18 months, he went from being in debt to owning multiple locations. "God didn't just restore the years," he said. "He fast-forwarded my purpose."

If you feel behind, forgotten, or delayed, take this to heart: God can make up for lost time. Don't stress about what hasn't happened yet. Stay aligned. Stay faithful. Acceleration is on the way.

DECLARATIONS:

Speak these with expectancy and faith:

- God is redeeming my time and accelerating my steps.

- I am not behind; I'm right on time in God's calendar.

- What others waited years for, God can release to me in due season.

- Delay is breaking, and doors are opening.

- I will reap where I have sown and even where I haven't.

- I walk in divine alignment and supernatural momentum.

- I rise into acceleration, increase, and overflow.

PRAYER:

Father, thank You for not being limited by human timelines. You are the God who restores years, redeems delays, and brings sudden favor. I declare that divine acceleration is my portion. Help me stay aligned with You so that when the doors open, I'm ready to walk through them. Let momentum, clarity, and provision flow. In Jesus' name, amen.

Day 26

BIRTHING
NEW THINGS

———⁂———

Scripture:

*"Behold, I will do a new thing; now it shall
spring forth; shall you not know it?"*

ISAIAH 43:19 (NKJV)

REFLECTION:

God is restoring old dreams and birthing **new
things.** Fresh visions, new assignments, and unseen
opportunities. Yet, like every birth, it comes with
stretching, pain, patience, and preparation.

The prophet Isaiah didn't say God might do a
new thing; he said **He will.** This means your best
days aren't behind you. They're forming, maturing,

and getting ready to break through. But here's the question: *Can you recognize the new when it doesn't resemble the old?*

Sometimes we cling to what was so tightly that we overlook what could be. God doesn't always bring revival through familiar channels. He might shift your career, change your relationships, or awaken a dormant gift. Don't fear the unfamiliar. Birth is rarely comfortable, but it always leads to new life.

A woman I know stepped away from her career to care for her mother, and in the stillness, God gave her a new vision. After her mother passed, she felt lost. But in that quiet time, God gave her a vision for a grief recovery program. She had never led anything before, but she obeyed. Today, that "new thing" is impacting lives in three states. Her assignment didn't die; it was simply waiting to be born.

What is God trying to birth in you? Don't resist the stretch. Don't abort the process. New things emerge when you say *yes* in faith and *no* to fear. You're not just recovering; you're **redefining.**

DECLARATIONS:

Declare these with bold expectation:

- God is birthing something new in me and through me.

- I will not cling to the old and miss the new.

- I say yes to the process, even when it stretches me.

- New vision, new favor, and new strength are emerging.

- I will not fear the unfamiliar; I embrace divine shifts.

- My future is forming, and I am ready to carry it.

- I rise into new assignments with boldness and grace.

PRAYER:

Lord, thank You that You are doing something new in my life. Open my eyes to see it and my heart to receive it. Give me the courage to embrace unfamiliar territory and the faith to push through discomfort. Bring forth what You've designed in heaven through me. Let new things spring forth, fresh oil, new doors, deeper purpose. I'm ready. In Jesus' name, amen.

Day 27

THE GLORY
AFTER THIS

~~~~~~~~~

Scripture:

*"And after you have suffered a little while,
the God of all grace… will Himself restore,
confirm, strengthen, and establish you."*

1 PETER 5:10 (ESV)

REFLECTION:

There's a *glory after this*. After the loss. After the
battle. After the silence. God never ends a story on
a low note. If it's still broken, still painful, still dark,
it's not the end.

The Apostle Peter experienced this firsthand. He
denied Jesus and faced public failure, yet Jesus

restored him. The broken one became the bold one. The failure became the preacher. The glory came **after.**

Some of the most powerful people I've met didn't quit during the "in-between." One man lost his wife unexpectedly and nearly walked away from his faith. But in his grief, he leaned into God. Years later, he began a ministry for widowers that now helps thousands. He told me, "I didn't think I'd ever feel joy again, but I've seen the glory after this."

You may not feel it right now. You may still be in the fight. But there is a glory coming that will wipe away the sting. God will restore you. He will strengthen you. He will establish you. And when it's all said and done, you'll be able to say, *"That storm didn't bury me; it built me."*

Hold on. God's grace is finishing what He started. There is **glory after this.**

DECLARATIONS:

Speak these with unshakable confidence:

- My story will not end in pain; God is writing glory into every chapter.

- What I've lost will be restored and multiplied.

- I will not be broken forever; healing is happening in me now.

- God is strengthening and establishing me through this season.

- I carry the hope of resurrection, restoration, and reward.

- This is not how my story ends; glory is coming.

- I rise into the fullness of all God has prepared for me.

PRAYER:

Father, I thank You that after this trial, there will be glory. I refuse to settle in sorrow. I lift my eyes above the pain and look toward Your promise. Restore what was lost. Confirm what You've spoken. Strengthen what remains. Establish me in faith and purpose. Let Your glory shine through my story. In Jesus' name, amen.

Day 28

GRACE TO FINISH STRONG

Scripture:

"I have fought the good fight, I have finished the race, I have kept the faith."

2 TIMOTHY 4:7 (NIV)

REFLECTION:

Starting is easy. Finishing—especially finishing strong is where the real challenge lies. It requires more than just enthusiasm; it takes grace.

Paul's words near the end of his life were not filled with regret or excuses. He didn't merely survive his assignment—he completed it with boldness. That's what God desires for you. It's not just about starting a business, a ministry, or a dream; it's about seeing it through to the end. It's not only about overcoming one obstacle but walking in victory through every season.

Finishing strong doesn't mean you didn't face struggles. It means you didn't stop. It means you got back up when you felt like quitting. It means you held onto faith when fear seemed easier.

I think of a young man who returned to school in his 40s after years of delay. Every semester felt like a mountain. With work, kids, and financial pressures, he considered quitting more times than he could count. Yet, he kept showing up. And when he finally walked across that graduation stage, tears in his eyes, he said, "This wasn't just about a degree. It was about finishing what I started."

God's grace is not just for your past; it's for your finish. When you lean into it, you'll find strength you didn't know you had. You're not just rising, you're rising to finish.

Don't slow down now. Don't back out. Grace is carrying you. Finish strong.

DECLARATIONS:

Declare these with prophetic confidence:

- I have the grace to finish strong.

- What I started in faith, I will complete in victory.

- I will not quit, stall, or give up.

- God is strengthening me for the final stretch.

- My finish will be greater than my beginning.

- I press forward with power and clarity.

- I am a finisher, not just a starter.

PRAYER:

Father, thank You for the grace to begin—but even more for the grace to finish. I refuse to give up halfway. Strengthen my hands, fuel my spirit, and steady my heart. Help me to complete what You've called me to. Let my life be a testament to endurance and faith. I receive grace to finish strong, in Jesus' name. Amen.

Day 29

LEGACY, NOT
JUST SUCCESS

Scripture:

"The righteous man walks in his integrity; his children are blessed after him."

PROVERBS 20:7 (NKJV)

REFLECTION:

Success is what you achieve; legacy is what you leave. In a world chasing recognition, God seeks those who will build something that outlives them.

The risen life is not just about rising for yourself; it's about lifting others. What good is a breakthrough if it ends with you? What if your rise was never meant to be private, but generational?

Legacy isn't always loud; it's not about fame. It's about faithfulness. It's the quiet decisions to live with integrity—obeying when no one's watching, discipling your children, mentoring others, and serving with excellence. You don't need a big platform to leave a big impact.

A woman in her seventies never preached a sermon, yet her funeral overflowed with testimonies of her impact. Yet at her funeral, dozens stood to say how her prayers, encouragement, and generosity changed their lives. Her children, grandchildren, and spiritual sons and daughters all carried her faith forward. She didn't just live well; she left a legacy.

Don't just aim to rise; aim to reproduce. Pour into others. Write the book. Share the wisdom. Raise sons and daughters in the Spirit. Let your life echo beyond your time.

You were not born to be impressive; you were born to be impactful. The goal isn't to be remembered for what you did, but to be followed for how you lived.

DECLARATIONS:

Say these with intentionality and vision:

- I choose legacy over popularity.

- My life will outlive me in impact and purpose.

- I will raise up others as I rise.

- I live with integrity, faith, and eternal perspective.

- God is using my life to bless generations.

- My ceiling will be someone else's floor.

- I rise with a legacy mindset.

PRAYER:

Lord, help me to think beyond myself. Don't just make me successful; make me impactful. Show me who to mentor, how to serve, and what to build for the next generation. Let my life count for eternity. May I be remembered not for my titles but for my testimony. Use me to leave a legacy of faith, love, and purpose. In Jesus' name, amen.

Day 30

RISE AGAIN, FOR GOOD

Scripture:

"For though the righteous fall seven times, they rise again..."

PROVERBS 24:16A (NIV)

REFLECTION:

You've made it to Day 30, but this is not the end. It's the beginning of a new rhythm, a new mindset, a new lifestyle. Rising is no longer just an idea; it's who you are.

This journey wasn't about temporary hype; it was about divine transformation. You've confronted fear, shame, regret, delay, resistance, and doubt.

100

And now, like a warrior coming out of the fire, you rise. Not with scars alone, but with **strength.**

Proverbs doesn't say the righteous never fall; it says they *rise again*. Your righteousness isn't proven by perfection; it's revealed in your refusal to stay down.

A man once shared how opening his Bible after deep failure became the turning point of his life. He lost his marriage, his business, and nearly his mind. But one day, he opened his Bible and read, "You will arise and have mercy…" That word ignited a fire within him. Today, he leads a recovery home for men coming out of addiction and homelessness. His life shouts: "I rose again, and this time, for good."

You may still face challenges, but now you rise **with wisdom.** You rise **with faith.** You rise **with fire.** This isn't the end of your rise; it's the launch into legacy.

Don't just have a resurrection moment; live a resurrection life.

DECLARATIONS:

Declare these with finality and fire:

- I have risen, and I will not return to who I used to be.

- I carry resurrection power into every area of my life.

- I rise daily with faith, focus, and fire.

- I will not be defined by my falls; my rise will know me.

- The past is behind me; purpose is in front of me.

- I live the risen life, full of power, purpose, and legacy.

- I rise again, for good, for God, and for glory.

PRAYER:

Father, thank You for walking with me through this journey. I declare that my rise is not seasonal; it is permanent. I won't go back. I won't shrink. I won't settle. By Your grace, I rise again and again and again. Let my life reflect Your power, Your glory, and Your goodness. Let others rise through my testimony. This is not the end; it is the beginning. In Jesus' name, amen.

www.ingramcontent.com/pod-product-compliance
Lightning Source LLC
Chambersburg PA
CBHW061700120626
46550CB00003B/1029